For Joan,
who knows all my secrets
but doesn't tell.
With Love,
Nora

STRONGER IN THE BROKEN PLACES

ISBN: 9781329002111

First Edition: May 2023

Stronger in the Broken Places

Dora Siemel

Dedication

*To the Wolf of my dreams who came into my life
long after I had quit believing in him.*

A Heartfelt Thank You

To my children Edith Malin and Michael Malin who were the bright lights through the darkest times and the best times.

To my grandchildren, Xander Malin and Jillian Malin who have filled my life with sparkling joy and unimaginable love.

A Very Special Thanks

To Nicole Pollard who created the wonderful cover page and put this book together for me. This book would not have happened without you.

Table of Contents

Stronger in the Broken Places

After love or war or hurt
take time to lick your wounds and rest
find silver linings in black clouds
everything is for the best.

Glorious fading remnants
can inspire and can console
ruins can be more beautiful
than the once unbroken whole

I have hurt and lost and failed
adversity has many faces
and though they ache when it rains
I'm stronger in the broken places

1978

Love Or Something Like It

*If you can manage it without collapsing into a heap
of cognitive dissonance, then try the unthinkable:
gratitude, not for the betrayal but for the do-over
opportunity.*
– Carolyn Hax

Severing a relationship is one way of making peace.
- Carolyn Hax

*At a concert of Mongolian throat singers, someone attending thought the songs all sounded
sad. When a Mongol singer was asked what the songs were about, the answer was "Our
songs are about the same things that everyone else's are about: lost love or somebody stole your
fastest horse."*

MY PRETTY RED BUFFOON

You burst my pretty red buffoon
You rained on my charade
I planned to love you always
And I would have if you'd stayed

So lift on high the feathered flagon
toast new beginnings as we part
Take the promises you made me
and burn them on your flagstone heart

Shattered like a crystal goblin
broken like a glass mirage
I took the largest shining pieces
and made a stunning life collage

1979

MEXICO

All the days in Mexico
are hot and clear
or wet and slow
All our golden times are gone
but golden traces linger on

Now when my days are ice and snow
I close my eyes and then I go
wet and golden, clear and slow
back to Mexico

The evenings in Mexico
are soft and warm
The love is slow
Our silver nights just didn't last
memories linger, love is past

And when my nights are cold I know
I close my eyes and I can go
in a warm and silver flow
back to Mexico

The mornings in Mexico
are humid, warm
and have a glow
and so did you and so did I
then love went on and passed us by

Still when I'm sad or feeling low
I close my eyes and I can go
humid warm and all aglow
back to Mexico.

1974

LOVE IS VERY PAINFUL

I loved you but you left me
when your love had died
My world fell in, my life turned gray
and crumbled up inside

I would have given anything
just to make you stay
anything I owned or did
or cared for any way

Still I wish you all the best
the best to your new friend
Even though I loved you
Even through it had to end

Love is very painful
the pain goes on and on
Love still hurts all the time
ever since you've gone

I never want you hurt like this
I don't want your tears
So with all my heart I wish you both
many, many happy loveless years

1984

DREAMER

His hair poured down his shoulders
just like honey in the sunlight
and flowed like liquid amber
halfway down his back

He was a dreamer and a drifter
And a gambler and a poet
And now he's disappeared
Without a trace

He gave up his poetry
and his save the world dreams
His rose colored glasses
are smashed to smithereens

What is lost and what is gained
and what is thrown away
The dreams he'll never dream
and the songs he'll never play

But I remember hair like honey
in a wild and lonely place
that flowed like liquid amber
as it brushed across my face

1974

LADIES BEWARE

Ladies beware of innocent outlaws
and others whom fate casts astray
They'll tell you sad stories that tug at your heart strings
and you'll probably want them to stay

Their eyes may be blue as the mid-summer skies
or as dark as the pits of hell
They'll come into your life like the fourth of July
and soon you will like them too well

Ladies beware of all gallant highwaymen
beware virtuous rakes
They'll tell you they love you and touch you as gently
as if they think you might break

Their skin feels like velvet, their muscles like bones
they'll tell you they came from the gutter
They're cuddly as babies and friendly as puppies
and warm as sweet melted butter

Ladies beware of naive desperados
beware of woebegone strays
They'll show you their scars then smile like the sunshine
and leave you in sweet disarray

Their hair may be ivory and hang past their shoulders
or dark and curl round their ears
but fate preserve ladies from guileless gamblers
and swashbuckling mutineers

Ladies beware of beautiful bandits
beware of honorable thieves
they'll tell you that they were just innocent victims
then steal your heart as they leave

1982

I NEVER REALLY KNEW YOU

I never really knew you
but for that little while
you made me feel beautiful
and when I think of you I smile

You knew my name but called me Lady
I felt lucky all night through
You said every man in Vegas
looked at me and envied you

If what we had was wrong or bad
then why did I feel lovely all the while
If knowing you was wrong or sad
then why do I think of you and smile

We danced and loved and gambled
and won two out of three
and everything was right and good
so smile when you think of me

1975

I DON'T UNDERSTAND

I don't understand
and I guess I never did
what it was you ran from
or why it was you hid

I only know I loved you once
and it hurt when I did
I just never understood
why you ran and why you hid

I wish you every happiness
I'm always on your side
and I hope you think well of me
when you no longer run and hide

But I don't understand
and I guess I never will
why you ran and hid from me
or I'd be with you still

1982

HELLO MARI

Hello Mari,
How are you, I'm fine
I called to thank you for the party
Did I have a good time

Did I play my guitar
Did I get pretty stoned
Did I insult anybody
And how did I get home

Did I dance on the table
Did I take off my clothes
Did I tell any secrets
Just what did I expose

Did I hug everybody
Did I kiss two or three
and who's the pretty blonde
I just found in bed with me

Is he someone you know
Is he over twenty-one
I'd hate to be arrested
When I don't recall the fun

FORGETTING

Do you take cream in your coffee
oh that's right you drink tea.
I'm forgetting you by inches
and you're forgetting me
Remember the fun we had
when we painted this old town,
the laughter in your eyes of blue
that's right your eyes are brown

It's a very small forgetting
like fog instead of rain
a gradual numbing
instead of sharp pain
It's happening so slowly
as if it was meant to be
I'm losing you by inches
and you're losing me.

Would you like a martini
or do you prefer wine
I'm sure I used to know
long ago when you were mine
You know the beach where
we made love in Acapulco Bay
That's right it wasn't you
there with me that day

Do you take cream in your coffee
oh that's right you drink tea
I'm forgetting you by inches
and you're forgetting me
I'm losing you by inches
and you're losing me
I guess that's how love goes
and how life's supposed to be

1977

EYES THE COLOR OF EMERALDS

Eyes the color of emeralds
happy in your arms I lay
I just wanted to love you
but you just wanted to play

Eyes the color of emeralds
I wanted you to start each day
but all you wanted was laughter
and any excuse to play

A dreamy nineteen I fell in love
but you would have your way.
You looked down from your thirty six years
and said you wanted to play

Eyes the color of emeralds
well every dog has his day
You've come back and want my love
and I just want to play

Eyes the color of emeralds
feet the color of clay
I just wanted to love you
but you just wanted to play

Eyes the color of emeralds
hair the color of gray
now that you're old you want my love
and I just want to play

1976

COME LIVE WITH ME

Come live with me you said
I'll let you be free
and anything you want to be

I said you offer nothing
that isn't already mine
without your permission

Thank you for your kind offer
would you like me to slip into some chains
to make you more comfortable?

1979

THE PLEASURE OF YOUR COMPANY

I don't want you cause I'm lonely
and there's nothing else to do
I want you cause I like the way
I feel when I'm with you

I don't want you cause I'm scared
and need a place to hide
I want you for your warmth
and the way you are inside

I don't want you for your money
or what you can do for me
I want you for the pleasure
of your company

YOUR PICTURE

Your picture is still on my desk
for the same reason
I left a half a pack of cigarettes in the freezer
when I quit smoking

1980

TRUST

Trust is a man-word
for something you give and he takes

Promises are precious gems
with good resale value

When he paints his dreams for you
forever is used a lot

Of course you understand
promises can't always be kept

And forever isn't very practical
and generally he leaves you standing

knee-deep in trust

SOMETHING

I can't tell you what I feel
put a name to it
I can only tell you that
it's soft
and warm
and good
and hard
and misty
and crystal clear
and many other things
but I don't know what to call it
and it doesn't seem to matter

1979

A DANCE

a dance
or three
and nothing more
entranced
we linger on the floor
and search for words to say
before the music stops
and the band packs up
and goes away

1979

STRAWBERRY WINE

With loving and wanting and hugging and such
sometimes it gets scary to like you so much
You're laughter and showers and fun and sunshine
and a hint of gardenia in strawberry wine

Blue eyed and suntanned and warm to the touch
sometimes it gets scary to want you so much
your head on my pillow we lie intertwined
like a hint of gardenia in strawberry wine

You're beautiful, perfect not a thing to retouch
and sometimes it's scary to like you so much
You're a friend and a lover a brother of mine
you're a hint of gardenia in strawberry wine

With echoes of springtime this summer is fine
like a hint of gardenia in strawberry wine

1979

THE ROAD CLOSES BEHIND US

The road closes behind us,
we dance to the music of time
I hope the top of your mountain
is worth the price of the climb

I know that the pleasure of loving
is not worth the price in pain
like carefully washing your hair
in radioactive rain.

What I've learned about loving and trusting
is painfully etched on my bones
Fierce ecstasy and warm company are repaid
with interest like loans.

The darkness mists around me
though the hurt may soften with time
I hope the top of your mountain
is worth the price of the climb

After your forever after
my moods change deliriously
The nether worlds of delusion
seem frighteningly real to me.

A puppet of ghosts and memories
the past is my fascination
I still hear you whisper impossible dreams
in tortured isolation

I hope the top of your mountain
is worth the price of the climb
If you get half what I've paid
you'll have pleasure rare and life sublime

1977

If you don't pay your exorcist you get repossessed
– Unknown

I wish I loved anything as much as my kids love bubbles
– Line from the move Knocked up

Don't believe the things you tell yourself late at night
– Cheryl Cole

TO A LOVE WHO HAS ERRORED

Pour a vial of ancient wine.
add elixir of serpent's bile
and quintessence's of dragon's blood
demons to summon and beguile

By these figures drawn,
by these spells enchanted
by unction of salamander and wolf
your will with mine supplanted

Gather Darkness, 'round me
tonight I cast a spell
bitter love into sweet hatred
hither and serve me minions of hell

Into the tapestried candlelight
an ocherous evil whispering comes
then 'neath blind unquiet stars
a ghostly pageantry of phantoms

Lurking madness of the soul
pushing the borders of sanity
in crags of wine dark vapor
writhing spirits beckon me

You were called to do my bidding
and thusly I command
Punish one who has displeased me
Listen well, accursed wretched band

Go slavering at his heels
through the depth and breadth of hell
Let him taste the bitter anguish
that I have known so well

Hate is a black river
Let him reap what he has sown
Let me hear the sound of his soul
squeaking bodiless into the vast unknown
Let fear stalk him nightly
Howling through his dreams

'til he flails and pleads and gibbers
in a black abyss of screams

I want him to know who sent you
so when he's cringing in hell
whisper my name, then write it in flame
and tell him once I loved him well.

1977

GOLDEN BOY

Lovely sad-eyed golden boy
not much time for fun
from oil field trash to millionaire
is a long an weary run

Golden boy with the golden hair
and drawl that shows your roots
with faded jeans and an cowboy hat
and thousand dollar boots

Golden boy with the golden tan
and a Texas taste for more
you turned into a lone star lover
when your golden belt buckle hit the floor

Dangerous angry golden boy
when the time to leave drew near
you threw your diamond studded watch
and chipped the chandelier

Golden boy with the golden laugh
it started out as a dare
and ended up with your diamond rings
tangled in my hair

Golden boy with the blue-green eyes
it wasn't much of a start
but it ended up with thoughts of gold
tangled in my heart

1980

24

VELVET

Velvet skin, velvet eyes
listen to my velvet lies
for truth and love have caused me pain
I will not tell the truth again
nor suffer love and agonize
just let me touch your velvet skin
and lick your velvet eyes

Velvet skin, velvet eyes
I come to you in lovers guise
in the comfort of your arms
I feel small and safe and warm
so hold me close and fantasize
while I touch your velvet skin
and lick your velvet eyes

Velvet skin, velvet eyes
through pleasure's haze I realize
that dreams like this do not come true
so we'll be dreamers, me and you
with reality our compromise
and I will touch your velvet skin
and lick your velvet eyes

Velvet skin, velvet eyes
can so easily hypnotize
this is a magic way to feel
nothing this good can be real
it's lucky I can memorize
the way I touch your velvet skin
and lick your velvet eyes

1979

ONE FOOT BEFORE THE OTHER

With one foot before the other
I make my way through life now
testing all my steps before me though
I know the earth's not crumbling
it only feels that way

The snow sifts softly downward
and I'm caught up in the falling
I get through the night by saying
I know that morning's coming
I put one foot down gently and,
if the ground will hold it,
put the other just before it,
though I know the earth's not crumbling,
it only feels that way.

The wind wraps itself around me
and mentions that I'm dreaming
but for all its icy breathing
it's still warmer than my soul is.
The morning greets me pinkly,
the terrors of night recede now,
leaving only fleeting shadows
that creep softly into daydreams
and tap me on the shoulder saying
remember night is coming.

But in the glow of dawning
I can bravely shrug my shoulders
and pretend I never knew them
and pretend they never touched me
but I know they're inside waiting
and only time will cure them
So one foot before the other
I make my way through life now
testing all my steps before me
though I know the earth's not crumbling
it only feels that way.

I tell myself brave stories
of others who survived this

and sometimes I believe them
when the sun has chased the phantoms.
If I get through one more night
now that much closer to forgetting.
In a year I will be smiling
wondering why I let you do this.
but for now I just endure it
and hope to see an ending
with one foot before the other
though I know the earth's not crumbling
it only feels that way.

The fires of love burn brightly
and leave very fine gray ashes
but someday I will remember
that it was you who caused this
and when that finally happens
and I'm free of all the hurting
you will feel snow forever
sifting slowly through your daydreams
and your nights will make you happy
to change to day's illusions
with one foot before the other
though you know the earth's not crumbling
it only feels that way.

1978

A SPECIAL KIND OF ARTIST

You never wrote a poem
and never painted one
You never tasted sunshine
and yet you are the one
who lets me write the poems
and lets me paint them too
and sunshine tastes like flowers
whenever I'm with you

When I fly I touch the sky
you skim along the ground
but I fly all the higher
for having you around
Come and learn and love with me
and I'll be your balloon
You can bring me back to earth
when I take you to the moon.

THREE LITTLE WORDS

I ache for the sound
of those three little words
that you haven't said in many a day
but to say them and mean them
are two different things
and I want you to mean
what you say

whether written or said
they'll go straight to my head
and doors will open for me
so answer my plea
say or write them to me
all that they mean can't have fled

I ache for the sound
of those three little words
that would open doors for me
and I would do flips
to hear from your lips
a heartfelt
"here's your key"

1979

BECAUSE YOU LEFT

Now I need some gentle silence
soft as the hiss of snakes or rain
fold upon fold of velvet quiet
to muffle this fierce and startling pain

1978

Critters

The Unicorn doesn't care about what makes theoretical physicists happy.
− Steven Weinberg, Nobel Laureate

Hunting is the only sport where the other team has no idea it's playing − Unknown

People who believe that god heeds their prayers have probably waived their right to mock people who talk to trees and guardian angels or claim to channel the spirits of Native Americans − Wendy Kaminer

THE WIND

My name is the wind and I sing to the cats
large and small, wild and tame
hunting marsh deer or rats

I sing to the tigers
that stalk the jungle night
I sing to the panthers, brothers of night

I sing to the lions and the ocelots
to leopards and cougars
cats with stripes, cats with spots

Jaguars and pumas, Siamese and lynx
I know where each sleeps
and I know how each thinks

I sing to the bobcats
house cats warm and small
They listen and answer when they hear my call

I sing to the cheetahs my name is the wind
They run with me, race with me
to see where I've been

I sing to the cats that walk the grassy plains
I sing on desert nights
and I sing in rain forest rains

I sing to cats in cages and on leashes restrained
to cats in apartments
long haired, short haired, maned
I snarl and I whine and they snarl in return
I call and they answer
I sing and they yearn

My name is the wind and I sing to the cats
large and small, wild and tame
hunting marsh deer or rats

1977

32

RUN WITH THE WOLVES

Last night I ran with a silver wolf in north Ontario
Felt the jolting in my shoulders when we hit the hard packed snow
Strange to run on four feet, feel moonlight burn my fur
howl into the whispering pines, then meet Diana and hunt with her

Diana with the champagne hair and blinding silver eyes
our lady of the wolves and stags, patient, strong and wise
Shall we run with the wolves, Diana, like shadows in the night
across an earth of ice and iron in every shade of white

A savage blinding blizzard erased our forest world
wind whipped snow like silver daggers all around us swirled
Deep within a snow bank I slept away the storm
while at my back a silver wolf curled strong and warm

Now I shake the snowflakes from my mind, think of bricks and steel
Try to walk and talk and work, forget how to feel
The four strong legs, the shining fur, the howling voice, were loans
but on my skin there echoes still a singing from my bones

WHALE HUNT

serene beneath the frothy waves
they danced and dove and dreamed
with gargantuan ponderous grace
immune to whims of time it seemed

in showers of dazzling splinters
they breached the cobalt sea
eyes would tear and throats would ache
at souls so wild and free

then came men in savage hordes
with implacable machinery
and red hell reigned rampant
in the shocked and stricken sea

iron men in iron boats
determined grim and strong
churned through the peaceful waters
that were not peaceful long

in the bright madness of slaughter
each harpoon an empty thud
before the shivering stars appeared
the sun set in a sea of blood.

silvery ghosts chant black dirges
under a sullen sleepless sea
mourning all those gentle souls
and our lost humanity

Arcane Anthology

*Meddle not in the affairs of dragons for you are crunchy
and taste good with ketchup
– Suzanne McMinn*

*The most haunted of houses is the human mind.
- Unknown*

*Not all those who wander are lost
– JRR Tolkien*

A BUBBLE

A bubble
clear
with iridescent rainbow highlights
floats on a stray breeze
dances gently
then disappears in a spatter
of parti-colored droplets
heart break city again

1979

BAR SCENE

A jumble of conversation
drifts through clouds of smoke
and leaves smudges on the thoughts
of silent drinkers
then dies on padded ceilings
and in marshmallow carpeting

1979

BATTERED

So many bruised
and battered lives
whose happiness is simply
the temporary absence of pain

1979

QUIET PLACES

In the quiet places between stars
sometimes a spaceling
howls its loneliness
across vast reaches of time
and yearning distances
and waits hopelessly
for a reply

1979

DARK VISTAS

Some sing of happiness and love,
draw flowers bound with silken cords
I yearn to paint dark vistas
and conjure ravening hordes

Cold stone brooding castles loom
with lurking danger, flashing swords
Heroes languish in vile dungeons
entombed by craven dragon lords

Ladies fair with ivory hair
proudly ride on blood red steeds
to rescue heroes from vile dungeons
and praise them for their mighty deeds

Boiling clouds in darkling skies
tattered by the shrieking wind
and thunder like the crack of doom
where stinging lightning forks have been

The sun sets in a crimson furnace
dry as the dust of wind-swept bones
The savage colors stir the dreamers
and the poisonous rage of serpent drones

Night comes down on shadowy wings
owls come ghosting by to jeer
Enchanted living dreams instill
a sweet and satisfactory sense of fear

A wise and ancient evil waits
out of demon nightmares from times untold
drawn by the lust for mystic rubies
and the pale cold fire of gold

The stars speak not of love to me
but rabid wolf packs, chanted spells
Insane moonlight burns my eyes
and summons demons from thirteen hells
I leave to others songs of love
of days like spring without a care

I toast you with a venomed chalice
and I tell you all I dare

DAYDREAMS

Garish apparitions
with apocalyptic pasts
edge into my daydreams
in a flurry of wings
and horns
and lashing tails
and
they please me greatly

1980

DESOLATION ANGELS

Desolation angels
on a desperation trip
ride the outer limits
of hallucinogenic clouds
Even with a mind sweep in this sector of the void
they will always be among the lost

1979

DIARY OF A SNOW WITCH

Once the sun poured down like honey
on the grass so warm and sweet
and the sand like broken diamonds
lay sparkling at her feet
Then she fell in love forever
Loved not wisely but loved well
When he left he took the summer
and icy crystal snowflakes fell

Now in turbulent dark vistas
gaunt flanked unicorns endure
Rhineland gnomes forge swords for heroes
and wild winds besiege the moor
In the thrall of iron winter
whispering forests darkly lie
and midst the smell of soot and brimstone
fragile faerie dragons die

Even winter has its beauty
crowned with jewel emblazoned snow
Ice is cold but pain is frozen
frost dulls the pangs of woe
and she remembers sun like honey
on the grass so warm and sweet
and she remembers sand like diamonds
once warmed her crystal feet.

1979

ECHOES

Listen to the winds of chance
that whisper through the caves of time
with gentle susurrations
that set the crystals humming
and reverberate with shattered light
on other planes than these

1980

MY DREAMS

My dreams are intricate affairs
The palaces adorned with
tessellated minarets
and oriental tapestries
and
Fearsome knights in burnished armor
nod gaily plumed helmets
and brandish ornate silver shields
and gem encrusted swords
while sunlight glints on
golden breast plates
heavily engraved with terrible beasts
both real and imagined
and
Pale ladies dressed in purple velvet
shot with strands of gold and silver
and embroidered with amethysts
and aquamarines
and other precious gems
and
Dragons trailing plumes of sulfurous smoke
dwell in jeweled caverns
or fly like armored birds
or drift on air currents like kites
out of some demon dream
and
Unicorns drink from crystal springs
and frolic with gryphons
and manticores
and minotaurs

FOURTH MANSIONS

Unicorns and dragons, peacocks and the like,
gargoyles gently lurking, clocks that gently strike
Candles burn in corners wild forests grow and bloom
Serenity and solitude in my fourth mansion room

Benevolent, beneficent quiet of every kind
hovers always near in the fourth mansion of my mind
I see my life through stained glass eyes
with amethyst shadows of paradise

This is where I live and this is where I'm free
here my head is barefoot and here I'm really me
The world cannot intrude for all the world is blind
and only I can see the fourth mansion of my mind

1977

WITCH WATER WISHES

Witch water wishes and magical fishes
play opulent crystal shells
Sand wizards dream and plot magical schemes
to the jangle of mystical bells

The sounds intertwine
with the taste of were-wine
in my home
and nobody tells

Trust beyond reason and Halloween season
cold as the teeth of hell
unicorn potions and dragonfly lotions
for a demon lover's spell

The sounds intertwine
with the taste of were-wine
in my home
and nobody tells

Wind weavers moan and ghost mourners drone
the thirteen names of hell
Dream dragons moon and mist faeries croon
the tales that forests tell

The sounds intertwine
with the taste of were-wine
in my home
and nobody tells

Demons cast runes, hum impossible tunes
and yell immoderate yells
while angels take wing and gloriously sing
midst the ominous tolling of bells

The sounds intertwine
with the taste of were-wine
in my home
and nobody tells

HOME

Welcome to the land
of byzantine fantasy
and
bizarre reality

1979

WERE-WINE

The moon above, the stars below
I fly, I need no wings
Horses soar and gryphons romp
and nightingales sing

The magic seeped into my life
by chance and whim of time with
moon-stained eyes and whispering grace
and cotton clouds to climb

You wandered out of your world
and stumbled into mine
where what never was has always been
like a taste of were-wine

With silken sheets of silence folded
round joy that burns like fire
the majestic and the crystalline
entwined in my desire

Gay banners fly from gilded towers
luscious fruit weigh down each tree
secret witches smile softly
with a touch of oddity

The faint rumble of a distant dragon
stirs memories of a star filled sea
before the magic traced my bones
with a streak of wizardry

Dazzling drops from perfumed fountains
explode like liquid dynamite
and dragons streak across the skies
and snack on weather satellites

You wandered out of your world
would you like to stay in mine
where what never was has always been
Have a taste of were-wine

1978

50

ONTO THE DARKLING PLAIN

Onto the darkling plain
from out of the darkling sky
like knights of old with banners bold
I hear them thunder by

Earth's bright terrible children
are coming home from the stars
riding on steeds of laser beams
with babies they've grown in jars

Swarming toward their home
across our skies they tear
with asteroid dust in their flashing smiles
and comet tails in their hair

Onto the darkling plain
from out of the darkling sky
wrapped warmly in their brilliance
our shining children flashing by

Earth your terrible children
are home from the stars at last
but do you want them and can you face them
them the future us the past

With eternity on their shoulders
they hear our baffling lies
and -I see the glitter of tears
and the glitter of death in their eyes

1977

51

Sanity Or
Something Like It

Life is not about waiting for the storm to pass, it's about learning to dance in the rain –
Vivian Greene

Depression is rage spread thin – George Santayana

A circle looks at a square and sees a badly made circle
– Jeff VanderMeer

DOWN THE RABBIT HOLE

Oh no, no
here we go
down the rabbit hole again

I love you, I am your friend
don't push me through the looking glass again
I am not strong, my life's not mine
I may never come back from wonderland this time

Mushrooms are tall
your bottle makes me small
I may never stop the fall
down the rabbit hole again

Right is wrong
but I'm your friend
The truth is lies
down the rabbit hole again

Oh no, no, no I have no name
I'm just a ball in your croquet game
I want to talk, to be your friend
Don't push me through the looking glass again

I am not strong my life's not mine
I may never come back from wonderland this time
You have one last chance to make amends
and you push me through the looking glass again

1973

IF YOU DO IT IN HOT WATER

Life is so wonderful
I've learned so many things
If you do it in hot water
it hardly even stings

I've learned everything important
at least that's how it seems
how to put out fires
how not to walk on dreams

How to say goodbye
how to do what's right
but not how to
make it through the night

I've learned how to love
and how to lose a friend
if you slit them vertically,
they're impossible to mend

Love is very beautiful
all the joy it brings
if you do it in hot water
it hardly even stings

I'll hold on as long as I can
and I only hope you'll see
I'm not doing this for someone else
but selfishly for me

Life is miraculous
but inside me something sings
if you do it in hot water
it hardly even stings

1974

SLEEP

I try to sleep
I lie in bed
My aching mind
My aching head
I long to sleep
a little rest
I fold my arms
across my breasts
I use my mind
to slit my wrists
At last I find
I fall asleep
and I am warm and I am free
with warm red blood
to cover me

1973

CLOSE TO THE EDGE

No one seems to know how close to the edge I stay
what a near thing it is for me
to survive another day

Falling, falling, falling, down and ever down
till falling takes my breath away
and gratefully I drown

The silver gray of moth wings
the dull white of eider down
threaten ever to enclose me in a filmy clinging gown

Deeper still and deeper, till I see the sky below
forever sighing downward
as I swim against the flow

The gargoyles take over
the cathedral is theirs and
nameless terrible dream monsters are stirring in their lairs

Falling, falling, falling thru cold reptilian rain
better end with one bright flash of light
and one bright shriek of pain

Like bitter yellow brass burned by bright barbaric sands
my soul dances like heat lightning
my life hangs in jeweled strands

And no one seems to notice how close to the edge I am
how high the flood is raging
how tremulous the dam

1977

DOWN TO THE BONE

Let me see how far I've come
another soft spot worn away
down to the polished bone
I've made it through another day
but on borrowed time
another loan

Acid life and acid love
have scoured all the soft spots clean
down to undissolving bone
And everything I've felt and seen
has seeped inside
and turned to stone

Everyone still thinks I'm sane
but the feather edges of madness
softly touch my time alone
Softly brush the glistening bone
that's all that's left of me
and claim it for their own

1979

TRYING TO DRIVE ME SANE

This is for your own good they hastily explain
as they pick apart my fantasies
and try to drive me sane
Illusions, all illusions
they heartily proclaim
as they break all my balloons
and try to drive me sane

Reality is dark and grim
clouds make silver linings dim
Rainbows cannot leave the ground
with pots of gold to weigh them down
My bones ache at their kind concern
their steel smiles and brittle eyes
the truth behind their guilt-edged lies

Let me weave my dreams in peace
with scintillating motion cease
all their finely tuned distortions
and their clever mis-proportions
and into sparkling webs of joy
their fragile verities transpose
Some emperors really have new clothes

They don't mean to be unkind
deaf to screams of wounded minds
Silent lobsters boil to death
not a sound with their last breaths
I'm told they feel no pain at
all going to their last rewards
They also have no vocal cords
Threads of fear wind through their souls
at what they see but can't control.
Insanity has wings and tails
life without the safety rails
Death a form of astronautics
I won't walk if I can fly I'll live forever or I'll die
Their feeling good is bad refrain
will never serve to drive me sane

REACH

Thunder rips the sky apart
and the pieces fall as rain
for some it means growth
for others it means pain.

It seem that some are born to take
and others are born to give.
I wonder if it hurts to die
as much as it does to live.

I know that once I reached for the stars
and once I dreamed of the sea
And I think that once the stars reached back
and the sea dreamed of me.

1980

TRAPPED AGAIN

too tired to run
no place to hide
they're coming at me from every side
just when I thought I could win
here I am
back to the wall
trapped again

1978

THE VOICES IN MY HEAD

Sometimes I like to lie in bed
and listen to the voices in my head
other times I tell them no
try to make them understand
it's my head
leave me alone

2015

Life Or Something Like It

*The more you ask life to grace you with improbable
things such as perfection at a catered event involving
alcohol and family members, the more gleefully life
giggles as it barfs on your dress.– Carolyn Hax*

*Death is not a medical event, but a natural one. In a
symmetry that would be elegant were it not so sad,
it is exactly as commonplace as birth. - Stephen P. Kieman*

*Some places remain unknown because no one has ventured forth. Others remain unknown
because no one has ever come back. – Despair, Inc.*

*The following was written by Rob Wilkins, Terry Pratchett's assistant after his death from
early onset Alzheimer's:*

*"At last, Sir Terry, we must walk together.
Terry took Death's arm and followed him through the doors and onto the black desert under
the endless night.
The End"*

A DEATH

All I cared was not enough
to keep you living on
and all I grieve is not enough
to let me know you're gone

Even as I cry and cry
I keep expecting you
to come and hold and comfort me
for all that I've been through

I see you getting out of cars
and walking down the street
but when I rush to catch you
into strangers you retreat

I love you, love you, love you
can't forget you but I must
or drift my tattered soul
between the stars like dust

grief as deep as the sky
but without a speck of light
how could you die and
leave me alone

terrified of night

1970

WHAT IT REALLY MEANS

Some say that he's passed away
others say he's gone
some even say he's traveled on
but my head is pounding and
and my heart is filled with dread
because no matter how they say it
it means my friend is dead

Some say that he's left this earth
he's gone to his reward
some say God has taken him
he's gone to meet his Lord
but my mind is churning
and my heart is filled with dread
because what they're really telling me
is that my friend is dead

There were some fatalities
at least that's what I read
he was among the casualties
so the reporters said
but inside me something screams and screams
my hopes have turned to lead
because what that really means
is that my friend is dead

1970

I WANT TO BE A MACHINE

I'm tired of broken promises, I'm tired of broken dreams
I'm tired of broken hearts, I'm tired of human schemes
I don't want to be angry, I don't want to be mean
I don't want to be human, I want to be a machine

I'll sing songs of energy in sweet and silver tones
my body warmed by copper coils wrapping silver bones
I'll sip high grade motor oil as you sip your wine
And my perfect saran hair will brush my stainless-steel spine

The circuits of my nerves, sensors of my ears
know the cybernetic taste of stars, the wailing of light years
I'm tired of broken promises, I'm tired of broken dreams
I'm tired of broken hearts, I want to be a machine

My thoughts will flare on micro chips and unlike my counterpart
a platinum compressor will cool my crystal heart
Flawless skin, steel nails, an iridescent smile
X-ray eyes and oiled grace and programmed sense of style

No more sickness, no more pain, no more broken hearts
Just effortless efficiency and new replacement parts
No more broken promises, no more broken dreams
No more broken hearts, I'll be a machine

1981

FOR MY MOTHER

When I was a child
I slept like a child
my life was free from fear
with magic from my Daddy
and my Mommy always here

When I was a girl
I dreamed like a girl
my future bright and clear
Christmas was my Dad
and my Mom was always near

Growing's good
but growing hurts
learning year by year
with emeralds from my Father
and my Mother always near

My Father died
the pain remains
life's better every year
and still when I need her
my Mother's always here

1977

THE DOOM SAYERS

They say my pinks will turn to gray
the glow will surely fade
my happiness is for today
tomorrow will be cold
They may be right
but
I'll have my memories
and they will have
I told you so's

A FAVOR

When I feel the stars like pin pricks on my skin
and something plucks at me to loosen bonds of flesh
I will need your strength to moor me to this plane
If you will be my anchor then
I will return the favor when
you have your own personal reasons
to scream and float away
and scream again

1984

LIFE WISH

I feel the stalking tread of time
fearful and weary past all knowing
It is not supposed to end like this
slowly and in pain
with knowledge burning through the pleasure,
a demon, horned with hooves of stone,
that grinds the flesh down to the bone.
To hurt is now to be alive,
to stop the pain is death.
Please stop the pain, I shriek
no!
what have I said
Please let the pain go on and on.

1970

A LESSON

What once was soft
has turned to stone
the truth has etched me to the bone
I know that I will die alone
and that has set me free

REALITY

Reality is grim
for those who make it so
my reality has wings
and frothy clouds
and sparkling snow
and an occasional dragon
with iridescent pink scales
just for show

A NEST

A nest of dreams
and fantasies
where the harsh edges
of the world
blur to velvet
and caress me
I am home

WHAT I'VE LOST

Sometimes through the fog I see
with icy crystal clarity
all I've done and loved and lost
like a ghostly parody
a shadow passing quietly

I am bereft no longer me
but deep inside there is a glow
a haunting tune
I used to know
and usually it comforts me.

2016

SOMETIMES I WALK THROUGH YOUR WORLD

Sometimes I walk through your world
Mostly, I stay in mine
Yours is dark and scary
and I stumble all the time

I've done my share of hurting
and sometimes I have cried
just to keep from screaming
when the fear wells up inside

How can I know so little
when I have come so far
It's a very private thing
between me and my guitar

I SING THE LIFE I LIVE

I sing the life I live
and I sing the way I feel
I sing all my dreams
and singing makes them real

When I feel happy
singing makes it stay
and when I'm feeling sad
singing makes it go away

When my world turns empty
I tell it in a song
and when I've been hurt
I sing away the wrong

I sing the live I live
and I sing the way I feel
I sing all my dreams
and singing makes them real

1977

Y CHROMOSOME SYNDROME

Muscle their problems
or leave them to luck
too dumb to stop
too brave to duck

1977

SCARS

Raw and ragged edges
drip gore
and weep clear liquid
then
finally heal into scars
like twisted crimson snakes
that fade to silvery snail tracks
with time

1974

EVERYTHING

Everything I am
or
was
or did
or loved
you stomped on and defiled
as if those things were me
You thought I was completely crushed
You thought I'd have to stay
How surprised you must have been
when I finally walked away

1974

A SURPRISE

Surely I must leave a
a trail of blood
where I have been

The blood must gush in spurts
not drip from wounds so deep
In such quantities it surely splashes
and splatters everywhere

I know that I will die
but then I don't
and I'm surprised

1973

The Omniverse

An eye for an eye makes the whole world blind
– Ghandi

You don't always find what you're looking for,
but you don't randomly find nothing.
- Lisa Randall, Cosmologist

THE SPACE BETWEEN ATOMS

A lot can happen in the vast spaces between atoms
Atoms themselves
are more like shark nets
than sieves

Things could easily slip through the spaces
and never disturb the pattern
It's not surprising things get lost
go missing
disappear

Some say they walk through walls
rather than disbelieve
I just wonder why
everybody doesn't

I'm a bit puzzled by floors
and walls
and
furniture

I don't understand why everything
doesn't fall into
a primordial soup
of atoms
or
something
smaller

2020

MISSIONARY

An unidentified missionary
from the vast spaces between galaxies
died in a stupid accident
on a freeway outside Culver City, California
Her unclaimed body
badly charred
was buried in a paupers grave
and no one knew
or cared

1980

STARS

The stars speak glibly of millennia and aching distances
I reach for them with yearning mind
and trace their patterns with my soul
I know it is their past I see
their long forgotten light
still they warm and comfort me

1980

THRESHOLD

At the threshold of the whirlwinds
something is singing siren songs
to long forgotten moonlets
and pock-marked asteroids
in the immeasurably empty spaces between stars

THE WINDS OF CHANCE

Listen to the winds of chance
that whisper through
the caves of time
with gentle susurrations
that set the crystals humming
and reverberate with shattered light
on other planes than these

1979

Spaceship Earth

Being in politics is like being a football coach.
You have to be smart enough to understand the
game and dumb enough to think it's important.
– Eugene McCarthy

Patriotism is often an arbitrary veneration
of real estate above principles.
– George Jean Nathan

Graveyards are filled with indispensable people
– Unknown

Only the dead have seen an end to war.
– George Santayana

FIGHTING SUPERSTITION

In fighting superstition
they're doing pretty well
but since they got the devil,
I hear hell has gone to hell

Where have all the were-wolves gone,
does anybody care
that there's no place left for goblins
or strands of angel hair

They put wooden stakes through vampires' hearts
and still nobody mourns
They burned up all the witches
and chained the unicorns

They've cleared trolls from under bridges
chased dragons from their caves
And now I hear that all the ghouls
are gone from all the graves

Did you ever wonder what they did
or wonder where they went
They all went into politics
And one was president.

1980

When great men make blunders, they count their losses in pride, reputation and glory, the underlings count their losses in blood. – From Battleship Sailor by Theodore Mason

The difference between mechanical engineers and civil engineers is that mechanical engineers build weapons and civil engineers build targets – Unknown

A politeness you might observe when dealing with a Politian belonging to a country that has nuclear weapons and a carefree approach to their deployment.
– Terry Pratchet

The death of man is a tragedy, the death of a million is a statistic. – Joseph Stalin

Old soldiers never die, only young ones – Unknown

LOVE

Love of country has caused war
love of god, martyrs galore
yet you say you love me

Duels fought for love of ladies fair
broken hearts for love's despair
yet you say you love me.

Love of power causes tyranny
love of food is gluttony
yet you say you love me

For love of honor bombers fly
for love of fur the seals die
yet you say you love me

Science loved by the megaton
battles loved by those who won
yet you say you love me

Fish are hooked for love of sport
love of justice ends in court
yet you say you love me

Love of country has caused war
love of god, martyrs galore,
aren't you glad I love you?

ACID RAIN

Acid rains are drooling down
from phosphorescent pewter skies
and ululating sirens tell
of monstrous atrocities

Where city spires glittered once
curl orchids of cement and steel
where unimagined forces played
and worst of nightmare horrors came real

Glowing pools of liquid rock
like eyes of some malignant beast
turn clouds gold and malevolent
a holocaust without surcease

And acid rains keep drooling down
from phosphorescent pewter skies
and ululating sirens tell
of monstrous atrocities

Oceans boil like witches brew
howling winds torment the land
Chromosomes bend and break
things slither now which once would stand

Semi eternal rays collide
death with life's baroque detail
Centaurs, Sphinxes born again
only to twist and change and fail

And acid rains keep drooling down
from phosphorescent pewter skies
and ululating sirens tell
of monstrous atrocities

Gaiseric King of Vandals
would stop and stare with awe profound
a whole world pillaged burned and looted
a planet raped and hell unbound
Now when pale phantoms weep
wishing earth green once more

to comfort and console them
I tell them that we won the war

And acid rains keep drooling down
with dreary dull cacophony
and ululating sirens tell
of our splendid victory

You can't get enough of what you don't really want
. – Wayne Dyer

LAS VEGAS

Glamorous Las Vegas has plastic grass to mow
and all the neon flowers on all the plastic trees
nod and gently glow in the artificial breeze

you can ride a plastic barge
thru artificial waves
run by plastic body guards beating plastic slaves

what happened to the earth and sky
I wonder where the desert went
what's not covered with neon is covered with cement

somewhere there's firelight
and real winds that blow
somewhere there's real rain and real rivers flow

all the stars along the strip
dim all the stars above
you can even rent a body and make artificial love

1975

A VISIT TO A NEWLY PURCHASED Mc MANSION

Nothing grows here
neither plants
nor minds
nor love
Upon careful inspection
the reason becomes clear
It's not the aftermath of a nuclear holocaust
or the result of increased sunspot activity
or even the death curse of Jivaro headhunter
It's simply
that nothing lives here
Acute post functional irrelevance is fatal to humans
it's just that they sometimes don't notice
However it would make an excellent
nay, ideal
showroom for a dealership
specializing
in the sale of
previously owned luxury automobiles

1978

Fragments

Happiness is not a life without pain, but rather a life in which the pain has been traded for a worthy price . – Orson Scott Card

Even when the sky is heavily overcast, the sun hasn't disappeared. It's still there on the other side of the dark. – Unknown

I'D LIKE TO KNOW

Sad and scary
or wild and wary
how do my poems grow
with souls of stone
and spires of bone
and steel icicles
all in a row

1978

FORMULA

I take my life a day at a time
and sometimes hour by hour
screaming in pain
drenched with rain
or even feeling power
is easier a day at a time
and sometimes hour by hour

LOOM

The grief spinners have done their work
the pain weavers are back
nerves strung tautly on the warp
shuttles poised above the loom
grasped in claw-tipped fingers
that slice through the star-webbed sky
and intermesh the high tuned strands
that sing their agony
in exquisite tones
that please their raw and angry gods

I LOVE YOU

I love you
as I love the sunset
just as you are
and not only for me

1979

AS YOU WALK AWAY

If you have to
be my guest
turn your back and walk away
I'd rather be alone
than beg someone to stay

BLESSED BE

Moon that casts
thick shadows
and thin silver
we are one
we are all
the Moon and I
Blessed Be

1979

WE FORGIVE YOU

To err is human
to forgive, Devine
We forgive you

In deference to and in consideration of
our past relationship,
after prostrating yourself humbly
you may stand when in Our Presence

However, in view of your
considerable transgressions
and probable wish to do penance,
a short period of obeisance,
groveling,
foot-kissing gratitude
and other forms of self-abasement
would be
neither
inappropriate
nor
unseemly

SONG

Moon flecked or
Sun dappled
my wings beat free and strong
Rain drenched or
storm battered
I endure and I belong
then sing it
and
revel in the song

1979

LOVE WAS

Love was a drear dim desert
where hearts gathered silverfish and dust
the very thought coldly daunting
Safer monochrome rainbows and lust

In a whim of time I found you
and hope, which springs eternal heaven knows,
glimmered like a wavering marsh-light
then like burning plumes of sunrise, rose

I was terrified to love you
hard shells shelter soft beasts
but you offered clouds and moon-mist
and unimagined feasts

Grim armor put aside
the dreaming dragons purred
and love rang out like brazen hammers
and warmed the shivering stars that heard

The love you gave you took away
but liquid ghosts of it remain
and the warmth reverberates
with bittersweet refrain

I loved you as best I could
and I think you did the same
and I'm glad that I did
and I'm glad that you did
and I still warm myself by the light of your name

1980

SONG AND DANCE

You do your song and dance again
I give you one more chance again

You look deep into my eyes
And tell the most outrageous lies
You're so sincere I must believe

But now, my verbal acrobat
I look at you with eyes grown flat
That used be so deep with love

So forget the song and dance, my friend
It never will be right again

1978

APPEARANCES COUNT

I have always wanted to be
The sort of person who
looks as if she belongs in a Rolls Royce
and whose emerald rings
seem to grow out of her knuckles

1979

WHISPERS

The whisper of a shadow
on the downy edge of night
the moon a clever crescent
that mocks the waning light
the petals of the future
drop through the wells of time
and dust my fragile dreams
with a fantasy of rhyme

1979

FEAR

Sometimes I can't
look in your eyes
for fear I'll see
what's in your head
and it will be
the same as mine

1979

SAYING GOODBYE

Talking to you loving you
I guess I didn't see
but looking back I think that you
were saying goodbye to me

I don't know you at all you said
I probably won't like you when I do
and then you said goodbye to me
when I said goodnight to you

How I felt about you
seemed like magic pure and free
but while I was loving you and missing you
you were saying goodbye to me

Thinking of you made me glad
though I missed you constantly
and it took some time to understand
that you were saying goodbye to me

Songs or Something Else

Rescue the drowning and tie your shoe strings.
— Henry David Thoreau

To be a really committed specialist is to know a great deal
about almost nothing, with the probable sacrifice of
understanding even that.
— John Kenneth Galbraith

History teaches us that we do not learn from history
— William F. Buckley

When elephants fight, the grass suffers
— African saying

If you're going through hell, keep going.
— Winston Churchill

Books are many things: lullabies for the weary, ointment
for the wounded, armor for the fearful and nests for those
in need of a home.
— Glenda Millard

IF WISHES WERE HORSES

If wishes were horses
then beggars would ride
if dreams would come true
you'd be here by my side
But wishes are wishes
as beggars have known
and dreams don't come true
so I'm here all alone

Burn candles at midnight
and call you to me
cast spells and mix potions
from old recipes
If I had three wishes
I'd first wish for you
and use the others to wish
that the first one came true

Rub on a rabbit's foot
Knock on some wood
might not bring you back
but it might do some good
Starlight oh star bright
I'll try something new
First star that I see
I'll wish on for you
I'll catch a small leprechaun
to grant me a wish
collect four leaf clovers
and magical fish
toss pennies in wishing wells
and wish you to me
crossing fingers for luck
just might be the key

When I see a penny
I'll pick it up
And hope that someday
I'll have better luck
Well, something is working
This is my lucky day

There's a beggar on horseback
And he's heading my way
And if wishes are horses
And beggars can ride
Dreams might come true
And bring you back to my side

Yes, look carefully and listen
It's my lucky day
There's a beggar on horseback
And he's riding this way

And if wishes are horses
And beggars can ride
Dreams might come true
And bring you back to my side

DIAMOND CUFFLINKS

His hair is gray and thinning at the temples
Even tailored suits can't make him thin
His butler says he cuts a dashing figure
But money can make the eyes grow dim

Her golden hair reflects the golden candle glow
She has cost him more than a good sized French chateau
Her perfect body matched only by her perfect mind
She's beautiful and brilliant, what a find

And he wears her like her wears his diamond cufflinks
Another dazzling jewel to flash for all his friends
He's happy and he's proud of her beauty
Her silver laughter makes him feel young again

He takes her to all the finest places
On his arm she glitters like a gem
And everybody knows that he has bought her
And still she is the envy of everyone of them

And he wears her like he wears his diamond cufflinks
Another dazzling jewel to flash for all his friends
And if you were to ask anybody
They would tell you that is where the story ends

But

She has a pair of perfect emerald earrings
Gift from a former lover with holdings in Brazil
And her friends are all emerald green with envy
They wonder how she manages to bend men to her will

And

She wears him like she wears her emerald earrings
His chauffeured limousine is at her beck and call
He sends bouquets of roses and gardenias
He buys designer dresses that she wears to fancy balls

It is a match that's truly made in heaven
Built on love as anyone can see

He loves her for her wit and for her style
She loves him for his money and his generosity

And

He wears like he wears his diamond cufflinks
another dazzling jewel to flash for all his friends
and she wears him like she wears her emerald earrings
and that is where the story truly ends

THEY COME OUT FROM UNDER ROCKS

I've got men by the dozen
Men by the score
all the men I'll ever want
and many, many more
now it's sad but true
as anyone can see
what they have in numbers
they lack in quality

Because they come out from under rocks
and fall in love with me
Leave their bridges behind them
and fall in love with me
Buck off prince charming a
and fall in love with me
Climb out of their trees
and fall in love with me
Slither out of swamps
and fall in love with me
Climb off their lily pads
and fall in love with me

Others find true love
And feel no remorse
When they get the white knight
and I get his horse
Cinderella got her prince
for all the world to see
But all the mice and all the lizards and one big rat
fell in love with me

Because they come out from under rocks
Leave their bridges behind them
Buck off prince charming
Climb out of their trees
Forget about snow white
Slither out of swamps
Climb off their lily pads
And fall in love with me

About the Author

Dora was born in Mato Grosso (now re-named Mato Grosso du Sul), Brazil.

In addition to being a poet, she is a sculptor, a computer consultant, a martial artist and a yoga instructor. Her sculpture, *STRONGER IN THE BROKEN PLACES*, graces the cover of this book.

Some of her poems started out as songs which she sang and accompanied on her guitar.

She lives in Green Lane, Pennsylvania with her husband, Robert Wolfarth and a recurring series of stray cats.